# Sabrina's Sprinkle of Magic

Sabrina Mason Coles



BookLeaf Publishing

Presentation by *BookLeaf Publishing*

Web: www.bookleafpub.com

E-mail: info@bookleafpub.com

ISBN: 9789357440240

First edition 2023

*This book is dedicated to my mother Pearlene,*
*my Ancestors and the entire Spirit team. Ase'*

# ACKNOWLEDGEMENT

Thank you Ancestors and Spirit team. My children Michael, Mason and Mi'Kya thank you for being my inspiration and my reason why. My brother Brandon thank you for everything you do. Thank you to my entire family that has supported me. Thank you to my mentors Emme Rain @The Magical Mystic and Tasha Matrez @Spirit Knows Best. Special thanks to the Editors and Publishers of this book.

# PREFACE

This short poetry book came into existence while reflecting on my journey. I am sharing here my random thoughts and personal experiences. I hope to put a smile on some faces and encouragement during your own journey. Sending you all love and light.

# A walk through the shadows

As I walked through the shadows I heard a little girl crying. I picked her up and wiped her tears. I explained things to her she didn't understand. I held her so tight and close it felt as if we became one. That is the moment that healing began.

# You are enough!

You are enough!
You've always been enough!
Lots of times you felt like you were not enough.
You were enough!
You are enough and forever will be enough!

# Gratitude

Grateful for the many blessings

Received and the ones to come.

Abundance flows to me.

Tears of gratitude fill my eyes.

I've come so very far.

Thankful every step of the way.

Uplifted by gratitude in times of

Despair. I fill my heart with thanks

Each and every single day.

# The Storm

There is a terrible storm brewing around me.
No sight of the sun as far as I can see.

I close my eyes and quiet my mind.
An illuminating light is what I find.

The sun is shining so deeply within.
Here is where I will find my sun time and time again.

# I Give

I gave you love with no boundaries.
I gave you understanding.
I gave you my time.
I gave you healing.
I grieved.
I give myself healing.
I give myself time.
I give myself understanding.
I give myself love with no boundaries.

# Positive thinking

Shift your mind. Control your thoughts. Think positive.
I couldn't imagine how this works. How do you do this?
I tried affirmations, meditation, and focused more on my own happiness.
One day I happened to notice my cup of coffee wasn't half empty it was half full.
I didn't have a world of people that hated me. I had lots of people that truly loved me.
I was not poor or broke. I was in between funds. More money was soon to come.
Shift your mind. Control your thoughts. Think positive.

# That teen of mine

It's Monday morning and right on time.
Here comes that teenager of mine.

Mom, I can't go to school today.
I have the worst headache ever. I'm not okay.

My eyes are pink. I cannot see.
I'm coughing and wheezing. Please help me.

I can barely talk.
I can barely walk.

My stomach hurts. My back is in pain.
If I try to read my brain will go insane.

School is canceled sick teen of mine. It's a snow day.
Right on time.

This child did a victory dance with lots of shimmying and hopping.
Get dressed Mom, let's go shopping.

# Manifest it

I dreamed about it.
I thought about it.
I desired it.
I made a plan for it.
I put action to it.
I manifested it.

# Keep going

It's okay to cry. Tears cleanse the soul.
Keep going.

It's okay to have a bad day. This day will be one in the past.
Keep going.

It's okay to set boundaries. Healthy boundaries are necessary.
Keep going.

It's okay to feel overwhelmed. One thing at a time.
Keep going.

It's okay to take a break, rest and rejuvenate.
Just remember,
Keep going.

# Soul Food

The kids are arguing, fussing and complaining.
Accusations of charger stealing and earbud wearing are flying through the air.
It's time for food for the soul.
Honey garlic chicken.
While seasoning the chicken I give thanks and appreciation. As the chicken bakes, a pot on the stove is Sprinkled With Magic.
Butter and honey to sweeten our souls. Garlic and pepper to protect.
The chicken is placed in this magical mixture to caramelize.
We give thanks.
We eat.
The kids are smiling and peace is restored.

# Sprinkle of magic

Sprinkle some magic wherever you go.
Share a smile, give a compliment. Just let love flow.

Sprinkle some magic in the things you do.
Whatever you put out to the universe comes right back to you.

Sprinkle some magic.

# I am.

I am capable of giving and receiving love.

I am beautiful inside and out.

I am a magnet for money and wealth.

I am grateful I have everything I need.

I am healthy and strong.

I am peaceful and calm.

I am in the flow with my Divine Purpose.

I am.

# Teach them.

Teach them.
Please and thank you go a long way.
Love yourself child everyday.
No one is the same as you at school.
Being different is the new cool.
Just because you could,
Does not mean you should.
Nothing seems to be going your way?
No worries. Tomorrow is a new day.
Don't worry about what people think of you.
Be yourself. That's what you are meant to do.

# Haiku dedicated to fire

Fire opened roads
I see a much clearer path
Forward- step by step

# Haiku dedicated to Earth

My beautiful tree.
I felt healing and grounding.
You hold my secrets.

# Auntie

Thank you for choosing me to care for your little one.
I am called Auntie. I get the job done.

I'm a child magnet everywhere I go.
Little ones run to me with open arms. Even the ones I do not know.

I nurture, love and protect all children around me.
I'm sure that's the reason why they choose to call me Auntie.

When I leave, the Children Cry.
I will see you later. This isn't a final goodbye.

These babies become grown.
Having children of their own.

They are quick to call on me.
I'm a major part of the family.

My babies, Auntie loves you too.
I always will. No matter what you do.

# Peace of mind

Peace of mind is my goal today.
All negativity will be pushed away.

My body and soul connect with my mind when at peace.
All chaos around me is ordered to cease.

A healing white nourishing light fills my mind, body and soul.
Today peace of Mind Is My ultimate goal.

# Haiku dedicated to water

Water with bubbles
Understanding your meaning
Good or bad unseen

# When?

My spirit team confirmed it's for me.
I work my magic daily.
An energy shift was felt. What could this be?
Things began to look doubtful for me.
Be patient. Looks aren't always what they seem
to be.

# Haiku dedicated to Air

Air carries my words.
You fill my body with life.
Exhaling solace.

# Words hurt

Words hurt! They absolutely do.

No matter if said from anger or if simply true.

A sharp tongue can cut like a blade.

Causing a hurt and pain that never fades.

Be mindful of your words is what I am telling you.

Words hurt! They absolutely do.

www.ingramcontent.com/pod-product-compliance
Lightning Source LLC
Chambersburg PA
CBHW062111140826
49812CB00058B/1243